Relative

Disasters

Novels by Wilkie Martin

unhuman series

Relative Disasters

a little book of silly verse

by
Wilkie Martin

with illustrations
by Ade Gorst

The Witcherley Book Company
United Kingdom

British Library Cataloguing in Publication Data.
A catalogue record for this book is available from the British Library.

ISBN 9781910302088 (paperback)
ISBN 9781910302095 (kindle)
ISBN 9781910302101 (ebook)

The Secret of My Success first published in Graffiti Magazine in 2009.

Contents

Introduction

It is rare for me to write anything resembling a poem. It is even rarer for me to be so satisfied with the results that I consider one finished, and even then there is always scope for further tinkering. This short volume of silly verse contains a selection of those that have been sufficiently tinkered with to share. The first one I wrote in this selection was Bonehead. It started as a serious attempt at a short story (based on a tale my grandmother told me, which she believed was true), changed into an attempt at a serious poem, and finally mutated into what it has become.

I used to have an excess of fictitious relatives, but have thinned out their ranks somewhat during the writing of these poems. The fictional ones bear no relationship to my real ones, who are all lovely (except for one, who will remain nameless to alarm all of them).

It's great when a poem comes together. However, since it appears that I can only write the initial drafts when suffering from a fever and I have been healthy recently, it is a rare feeling. It may also explain the somewhat deranged nature of the subject matter.

I have been an admirer of Ade Gorst's cartoons for many years, since the days when we used to scuba dive together. We share a love of the ridiculous, so I was delighted when he agreed to produce the cartoons for this little book of the absurd.

WM

For Uncle Hedley: in Memoriam

My Uncle Hedley's shocking encounter with a bumble bee.

Garden plants, though seldom deadly,

did for poor old Uncle Hedley,

who, taking time to sniff the rose,

sucked a bumble bee up his nose.

Although it did not sting, it buzzed

and Uncle Hedley raged and cussed.

The tingling made him sneeze and cough,

which caused his glasses to drop off.

He knelt to find them, full of wrath,

and found them shattered on the path.

He picked them up but cut his thumb

and full of fury blamed his mum,

For Uncle Hedley: in Memoriam

his father, grandparents and kin
who'd passed these defects on to him:
short sight, gout and haemophilia,
some of which can surely kill ya.

As blood poured out upon the lawn
he thought of those who'd shortly mourn
for him. What a sad disaster!
Then remembered sticking plaster.

He hobbled to the house quite fast,
his mind set on Elastoplast,
but, limping through the garden peas,
his Levi's dropped about his knees.

He tripped and fell into the beans,
while damning his defective jeans.
And yet, it was an allergy
to pollen caused fatality.

Hay-fevered eyes could see no shed,

he stumbled in and banged his head,

stood on a rake upon the floor

and knocked himself right through the door.

He stamped and swore — he was manic,

no decorum in his panic.

Running blind can be a gamble.

Thus, he fell into the bramble.

Stuck fast there, he felt such a prick

from all the thorns — pierced to the quick.

That's how Uncle Hedley ended,

in a bramble bush, suspended.

For Uncle Hedley: in Memoriam

A Gourmet's Unhappy End

A cousin learns the hard way that carelessness in sheds can be costly.

A Gourmet's Unhappy End

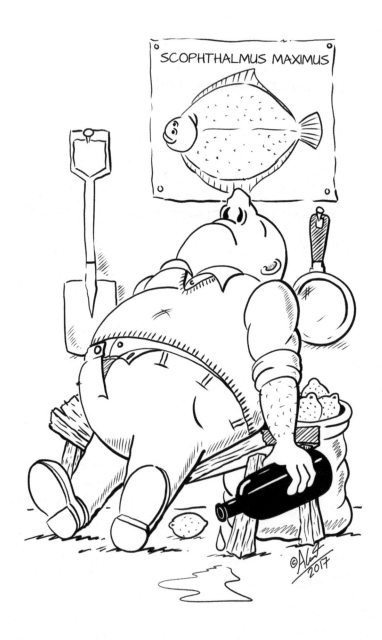

My lamented cousin Herbert

was a gourmet, fond of turbot.

And other fish? He would try 'em,

he'd gut and clean and then he'd fry 'em.

He adored fresh veg in season,

which he thought the perfect reason

to cultivate a garden patch

and complement the fishermen's catch.

It seemed at first he would succeed,

his crops supplied his every need,

his table groaned beneath the weight

of what he piled upon his plate.

A Gourmet's Unhappy End

Of course, he grew quite fat, I fear,

his chins wobbled from ear to ear.

Then one day, to his frustration,

there came an aphid infestation.

The dreaded plague of small green flies

began to spread before his eyes.

He tried a spray of soapy water.

Plants wilted still, despite the slaughter.

They faded, looking sick and pale,

he saw that his whole crop might fail,

and, falling into dark despair

he took to drink to ease his cares.

He wrote to Gardeners' Question Time.

They said, 'why not dig in some lime?'

His vegetables rotted from the roots

— they'd meant the mineral, not the fruits.

Wilkie Martin — Relative Disasters

He sat and sulked within the shed,

where he was known to keep, it's said,

his stock of weed-killer and drink.

He made a mistake, that's what we think.

He lay, a bottle in his hand,

an accident we understand.

Alas, my cousin Herbert died.

The inquest's verdict? ... Herbicide.

A Gourmet's Unhappy End

SCOPHTHALMUS MAXIMUS

The Secret of My Success

The happy outcome of my disastrous tea party.

This is a piece of pure nonsense and should in no way be regarded as a confession. My uncles are alive and well and living in Brazil. There never was an Auntie Sue.

My odious Uncle Michael once

kept a constricting snake

and when he brought it round for tea

it ate up all my cake.

We had some words, 'cause I was cross.

I said, 'that's not polite.'

And then it turned on Auntie Sue

and ate her in one bite.

I harangued the snake, most peevish,

'You shouldn't have done that,

Aunt Sue was very small and thin,

why not try Uncle Pat?'

The Secret of My Success

Pat looked askance and said, 'Oh no,

that's a daft suggestion.

Please don't eat me my serpent friend.

Think of your digestion.'

The snake's forked tongue flicked in and out,

it tasted Patrick's hand

but he'd washed in carbolic soap,

and didn't taste too grand.

Since Pat wasn't to its taste, it

started on the trifle.

I cried, 'Now, snake, enough's enough,'

and went out for my rifle.

Mike got down on his knees and begged,

'Please spare my little pet,

he's all I have, don't be so cruel.'

And my eyes grew quite wet.

But it was just a wicked ruse

to gain the snake respite,

for as I dashed my tears away,

it gave me such a bite.

I blazed away with erring aim.

I should have shown more care,

for I sadly shot my uncles.

I was their only heir.

That's how I became a rich man,

a gentleman of style,

and live a life of luxury,

all thanks to that reptile.

Was my tea party a success?

I find it hard to say,

but on my invitations now

I write, 'no snakes.' OK?

The Secret of My Success

The Man from Manhattan

A distant relative emigrated to the United States to expand his horizons and waist size.

The Man from Manhattan

An unhealthy man from Manhattan

would eat so much that he piled fat on.

He would pig out on pork

until, unable to walk,

he'd flatten whatever he sat on.

The Man from Manhattan

The Fatal Funeral of Uncle Ray

A terrible tale of tragedy and the risks of obesity.

The Fatal Funeral of Uncle Ray

Old Uncle Ray, an absolute glutton,

would stuff his face until he popped a button

or burst his zip, and he reached immense size

when he took to guzzling deep-fried meat pies.

He wouldn't see his greed was causing him harm,

pooh-poohed those friends trying to raise the alarm,

until the day when his belly had spread

and he could no longer get out of bed.

The doctor called round, suggesting a diet.

Ray just scoffed and said he wouldn't try it.

His life was in danger, the doctor foresaw,

yet never expected he'd fall through the floor.

The Fatal Funeral of Uncle Ray

Large lumps of lardy cake formed his last snack,

the joists gave way with a terrible crack,

and Ray dropped in on his sister Sarah,

who had been his most devoted carer.

Of her funeral, there is little to tell,

a sombre occasion, but all went well.

Yet his, the next day, was a disaster.

I can't think of many that were vaster.

The seeds were planted at the very start.

The undertaker played a major part,

for the man they chose was a black-clad creep

who conducted the funeral on the cheap.

On arriving, he gawped and stood aghast.

He'd never set eyes on a corpse so vast.

Throughout all his years, he'd never seen worse.

No way could he squeeze Ray into the hearse.

He stood for a long time, racking his brain,
finally deciding to call in a crane.
He'd seen one used to remove a beached whale
and had no inkling that his plan would fail.

He laid the departed out in a skip,
on moving, it started to swing and slip,
and as the cortege drove slowly through town,
fifteen pedestrians were crudely mown down.

Two dozen more fell on Cemetery Way,
twenty-four souls to join Ray in cold clay.
The undertaker rubbed his hands in glee,
as he thought of their funerals — and of his fee.

Ray's grave had to be so deep and so wide
that two of the diggers curled up and died,
while the one they left to complete the task
needed to breath from an oxygen mask.

The Fatal Funeral of Uncle Ray

By the time Ray arrived on his graveside,
forty-two innocent people had died.
In hindsight, it should have been a warning
of what lay in store for those in mourning.

The skip when lowered just dropped like a stone,
the shock shook everyone through to the bone,
the impact fractured the tectonic plate
and what happened next I can hardly relate.

The ground they stood on began to grumble,
the soil round the grave started to crumble,
the earth rose and buckled, clouds masked the sun,
some might have been spared had they started to run,

but they stood and grieved, the priest presiding,
and failed to spot the graveyard subsiding,
as out of the west a great crack appeared.
A hole opened up. They all disappeared.

Many folk perished, so it's said, the day

of the fatal funeral of Uncle Ray.

I'm only here, because I wasn't there.

Though he was family, I just didn't care.

The Fatal Funeral of Uncle Ray

Rebel Spirit

How my overactive great-grandfather got some wheels and went on the rampage.

It was only in his ninetieth year

that great-grandfather lost his fear

of what his dear mama might say

if he should ever go astray.

It was time to be a rebel.

Down with whist! And down with scrabble!

He needed something to his liking,

thought he'd take up motorbiking.

He got himself a suit of leather,

'Great,' they said, 'for any weather',

bought an old helmet from a mate,

thought to himself, I look real great!

Rebel Spirit

Black clad, he took the bus to town,
brows furrowed in ferocious frown.
Oh, yes, he thought, I've got the lot,
but there was one thing he'd forgot.

A motorbike! He slapped his head,
and hobbled to the shop and said,
'I want the biggest and the best.'
'Of course, sir! Have you passed your test?'

'Damn and blast, young whippersnapper,
sell me a bike, or I'll whack yer!'
But such threats failed to daunt the lad,
'I'll tell you what I'll do, granddad.

I do have something that might suit ya.
Why not try this lovely scooter?
It's good and cheap and painted black,
with skull and crossbones on the back.

It's got four wheels, so you can't fall.
It's got a great top speed and all
— eight miles per hour — but, they warn us,
not to lean too far on corners.'

He gazed at it and fell in love,
and helped the lad give it a shove
through the door into the alley,
paid in cash, and off he sallied.

Then began his reign of terror.
He'd scoot round Tesco all in leather
and everyone who was not quick
was prodded with his walking stick.

He lived to race between the aisles
and leave black skid marks on the tiles,
jumping the queues and living fast.
We knew, of course, it couldn't last.

Rebel Spirit

He thought he was beyond the law!
The manager first cursed, then swore,
'One day, my rebellious friend,
you will come to a sticky end.'

And, thus, he laid a trap, did Matt
(his name — I failed to mention that).
A cup of cooking oil was poured,
as round the aisles the scooter roared.

And Matt's staff raised a barricade,
closed every escape route and laid
in wait for poor great granddaddy
who, visor down, just could not see

the tragedy that lay ahead.
Towards the beer and wine he sped.
On hitting oil, his brakes quite failed
— a skid, a crash and off he sailed,

through bottles, jars and cans of Spam

and ended in a pool of jam.

Body broken, spirit lingered

long enough to raise two fingers.

And they do say, at dead of night,

the shelf stackers turn pale with fright,

in Tesco, still his favourite haunt,

as he rides out on ghostly jaunt.

Rebel Spirit

Bonehead

A mysterious visitor arrives in the night with tragic consequences.

Bonehead

Last night, as I lay in my bed,

a visitor stopped by,

a skeleton with grinning mouth,

who wielded a great scythe.

I froze as he strode up to me

but this is what I said,

'My heart beats, I'm alive and well,

I surely can't be dead?'

The hairs upon my scalp stood stiff,

as from electric shock.

'I think you should be dead,' he said,

'I'd better check the clock.

Oh! It seems I'm here too early,

Bonehead

enjoy your beauty sleep.

I'll leave your bedroom straight away,

I've other souls to reap.'

He grinned at me and clacked his teeth,

and said, 'Goodnight old chap,

I'll come for you around the dawn,

that's when life's thread should snap.'

I wrapped warm blankets around me

and covered up my head,

what I can't see can't hurt me and

I must be safe in bed.

My teeth rattled like castanets,

knees grew sore from knocking,

I pulled them up and hugged them and

sat there gently rocking.

I didn't get much sleep last night,

lying there in terror,

'til Bonehead returned at dawn and

said, 'There's been an error,

a little slip, an oversight,

I'm sorry for the mess.

It shouldn't be your time to go,

I've got the wrong address.'

He walked away but turned right back,

it's really not my night,

it might have been an error, but

I've gone and died of fright.

Bonehead

Acknowledgements

Once again, I would like to thank the members of Catchword for their support, guidance and encouragement over the many years that these poems have been in development: Geoffrey Adams, Gill Boyd, Liz Carew, Dr Jennifer Cryer, Jean Dickenson, Rachel Fixsen, Gill Garrett, Susan Gibbs, Derek Healey, Richard Hensley, Rhiannon Hopkins, Dr Pam Keevil, Nick John, Sarah King, Dr Anne Lauppe-Dunbar, Dr Rona Laycock, Peter Maguire, Jan Petrie and Susannah White.

I would like to thank Ade Gorst for his wonderful cartoons: they really bring the poems to life.

Writers in the Brewery and the members of Gloucestershire Writers' Network have also provided much appreciated support, and were kind enough to listen when I read to them.

Finally, a huge thank you to my family, who have put up with my humour for years, and to The Witcherley Book Company for making my publishing journey possible and for suggesting this collection.

WM

Also Available

Inspector Hobbes and the Blood

unhuman I

Wilkie Martin

'Odd, inventive, and genuinely very funny indeed'

Cotswold Life

For a sample of Inspector Hobbes and the Blood
tinyurl.com/unhumanI
or book2look.com/book/ZrFHGPVxgR

Inspector Hobbes and the Curse

unhuman II

Wilkie Martin

'far out fantasy full of odd characters and action'

The Book Faerie

For a sample of Inspector Hobbes and the Curse
tinyurl.com/unhumanII
or book2look.com/book/NqlwpcMhNm

Inspector Hobbes and the Gold Diggers

unhuman III

Wilkie Martin

'I enjoy how silly everything is.'

The Book Faerie

For a sample of Inspector Hobbes and the Gold Diggers
tinyurl.com/unhumanIII
or book2look.com/book/o8I6rbXQPo

Inspector Hobbes and the Bones

unhuman IV

Wilkie Martin

'I loved this. It's charming and bonkers.'

For the Love of Books!

For a sample of Inspector Hobbes and the Bones
tinyurl.com/unhumanIV
or book2look.com/book/6EJ4xgUg5Z

unhuman stuff

Unique designs based upon text selected from Wilkie's *unhuman* series of comic cosy mystery fantasies. Available on clothing for men, women and children: t-shirts, hoodies, sweatshirts, etc. as well as mugs, notepads, bags and more. Visit the shop on Wilkies website for details.

Design examples

Wilkie Martin

As well as these silly poems, Wilkie writes novels and now has four books in his *unhuman* series of comedy cosy mystery fantasies. The first of these, Inspector

Hobbes and the Blood, was shortlisted for the Impress Prize for New Writers in 2012 under its original title: Inspector Hobbes.

Born in Nottingham, he went to school in Sutton Coldfield, studied at the University of Leeds, worked in Cheltenham for many years, and now lives in the Cotswolds.

Sign up for his newsletter on his website to receive updates on his books.

To find out more visit his website or Facebook page.

wilkiemartin.com   tinyurl.com/WilkieMartinFacebook
            or facebook.com/pages/Wilkie-Martin-Author-Page/112466502150620

Ade Gorst

Ade has been drawing cartoons most of his life, in both an amateur and professional capacity. He has produced cartoons for numerous clients ranging from local businesses to the US Navy.

One of his first paid jobs as a cartoonist was a monthly cartoon strip in 'Dive' Magazine called 'Buster Lung' which ran for five years. Credit must go to the author of this book for coming up with the name in the early nineties.

When he's not cartooning he makes a living as a commercial diver, which has taken him to various countries around the world, from the oilfields of Saudi Arabia, to constructing underwater infrastructure for the 2012 Olympic Games in London and working in the movie industry.

To find out more visit his artist gallery or Facebook page.

ccgb.org.uk/gallery/showuser/adrian_gorst

facebook.com/BusterLung

A Note and Bear Advice from Wilkie

I want to thank you for reading my book. As a new author, one of my biggest challenges is getting known and finding readers. I don't consider myself a poet, and having read these you probably don't either! I do occasionally dabble and hope you enjoyed them: if you did I would really appreciate you telling your friends and family. A quick Facebook or Google+ status update or a tweet can make a difference, or if you want to write a review then that would be really fantastic. I'd also love to hear from you, so send me a message and let me know what you thought.

Thank you for your time.

Wilkie, May 2017

Bear

It's most unwise to shake a tree,
in case a bear falls out, you see.
And if you run away you'll find
it's draughty with a bear behind.

Relative
Disasters

Share a free sample from this book with your friends

tinyurl.com/wilkiemartinsillyverse
or book2look.com/book/Swm6RHTpTf

Lightning Source UK Ltd.
Milton Keynes UK
UKOW01f1350020717
304468UK00001B/139/P